# SHORT MAT BOWLING

# (2$^{nd}$ Edition)

## Roy Wiggins

**Visit us online at** www.authorsonline.co.uk

# An Authors On Line Book

© Roy Wiggins 2009

Cover design by Roy Wiggins ©

ISBN 978-07552-0448-9

Authors On Line Ltd
19 The Cinques
Gamlingay, Sandy
Bedfordshire SG19 3NU
England

This book is also available in e-book format, details of which are available at www.authorsonline.co.uk

## Previous publications
Some thoughts on the Game of Lawn Bowls 2002
Short Mat Bowling 2007

### Web Sites
www.miltonhill.go-plus.net
www.portcullis.org.uk

### Author's note
Following the success of the first edition, I have
taken the opportunity to add more detailed
information,  increase the number of illustrations,
and to revise some of the original text.
Enjoy your bowling!

**With grateful acknowledgements to:**
Rob Judson, for some of his basic data (http://www.robjudson.com)
Ernest Street, for his assistance with the pictures
Alan Ford, for his patience and help (http://www.onlybowls.com)
Barry Hedges,  Manager, England Short Mat Bowls Team for his
encouragement
Geoff Barnett, for crossing all the t's, dotting all the i's and making it
all easier to read (http://www.booksonbowls.co.uk)

| Section | Contents | Page |
|---|---|---|

# 1. Objective

The aim of this book is to introduce you to this fascinating sport, to offer guidance to the new player and to suggest some ways of overcoming difficult playing situations.

## A brief summary of the game

The objective of the game is simple: to get more of your bowls closer to the jack than your opponent.

The game is played as:
Singles. One player per team, 4 bowls each
Pairs. Two teams of two players, 2 bowls each player
Triples. Two teams of three players, 2 or 3 bowls each depending on local competition rules
Rinks, also known as Fours. Two teams of four players, 2 bowls each

All games are played to a specific number of 'ends', that is when all the players have bowled their bowls from one end to the other the 'end' is completed and the score for that end agreed. Every team has a skip who is totally in charge of his team. Details of the roles of each member of the team are described in Section 24.

When rolled up, the carpet measures about 6 feet wide by 2 feet across the diameter. When unrolled (Fig 1) it's normally called the 'mat' (but to avoid confusion with the 'delivery mat' it will be referred to as the 'carpet') and is between 40 and 45 feet long.

A white wooden block measuring 15 inches long by approximately 3 inches high and 2 inches wide is placed in its centre. At each end is a wooden fender that has an inside width of 6 feet with two 1 foot long, right-angled end legs. This is to define the limits and to provide some protection to the players, see Fig 2.

# 2. Carpet markings

## The layout at each end of the carpet

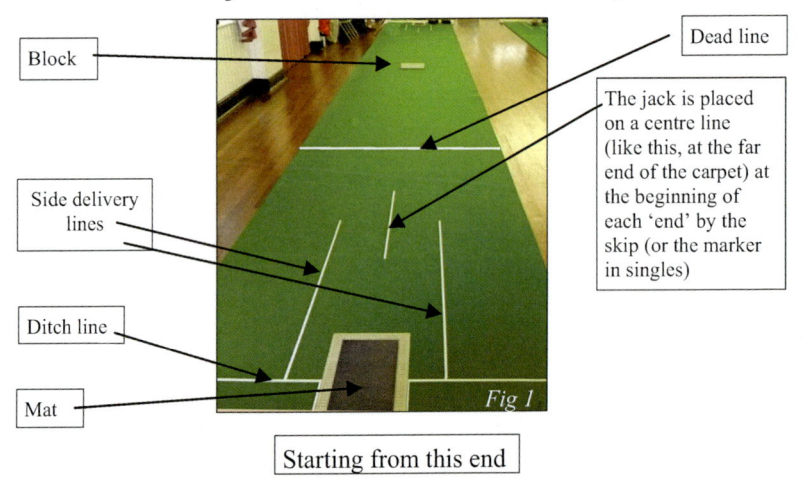

Block

Dead line

The jack is placed on a centre line (like this, at the far end of the carpet) at the beginning of each 'end' by the skip (or the marker in singles)

Side delivery lines

Ditch line

Mat

*Fig 1*

Starting from this end

## The determining part of the lines

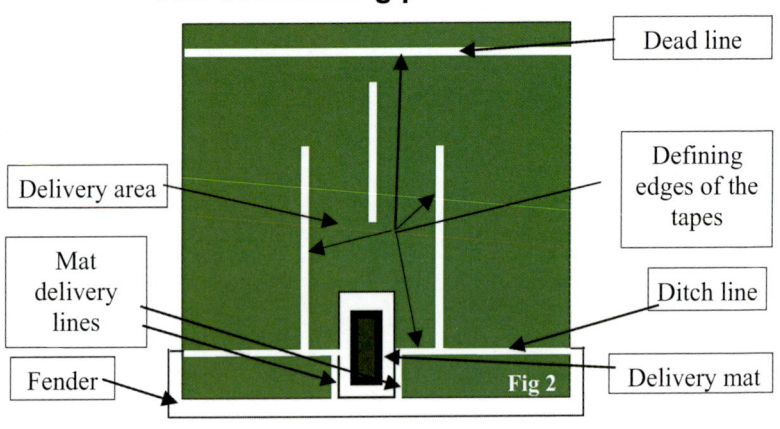

Dead line

Delivery area

Defining edges of the tapes

Mat delivery lines

Ditch line

Fender

*Fig 2*

Delivery mat

Not to scale

# 3. Some rules

The fender should be placed so that the ends of the right-angled sections are in line with the front defining edge of the ditch line tape. The delivery mat is always placed on the carpet within the mat delivery lines, at the start of each end, with its shorter end just touching the inside of the fender, which is there to protect the players and to define the limits of the playing area. If a bowl is driven over the fender, penalty points are awarded to the other team. The jack is placed on the centre line in a position decided tactically by the skip.

The bowls are often known as 'woods', but for clarity will always be called bowls in this book.

## At the beginning of the first end

A coin is tossed to determine who goes first. The winner of the toss will quite often put his/her opponents in first so that they retain the advantage of having the last bowl. The two skips then go to the other end of the carpet. The jack is placed on the 'centre line' by the  skip whose side is bowling first. It is part of the tactics of the game that the skip decides where exactly it is placed. i.e. a short, long, or an intermediate position.

In singles competitions the marker will place the jack according to the first player's instructions.

The delivery mat having been laid by the lead, all members of the team (except the skip) stand behind the fender, except when actually bowling.

## During play

When delivering your bowl you mustn't step outside the side delivery lines and you must have one foot entirely within, or above, the confines of the  delivery mat when you release the bowl.

You mustn't step over the nearest dead line until you've delivered all your bowls and generally only when your team or opponent is ready to move to the other end.

*All bowls that do not cross the far 'dead line' or that touch the centre block: or that touch or cross the ditch line, without first touching the jack: or are the result of a 'foot fault': are dead bowls, and are immediately removed from the playing area.*

The exceptions to this are skips and sometimes threes, prior to delivering their last bowl in an end, but this depends on local rules.

If the jack is driven off the carpet, rebounds or is deflected into the 'dead area' (that area between the two dead lines) the end is dead and must be replayed from the same end as before.

During a match, it's usual to allow two or sometimes three such dead ends per team without penalty.

If you deliver a bowl that touches the jack, either directly or indirectly off another bowl, it becomes a 'toucher' and should be clearly marked with chalk by a member of your team before the next bowl comes to rest.

If the jack is driven into the ditch (the area between the ditch line and the fender) it remains 'live' and can't be moved except by a toucher. If, whilst in the ditch, it's displaced by a subsequent non-toucher bowl, it must immediately be restored to its original position by the opposing player in charge of the head at that end and the non-toucher removed.

If part of a toucher protrudes over the ditch line into the playing area it is deemed to be live and can legitimately be struck by a non-toucher. If part of a jack protrudes likewise, it is also live and can be struck with a delivered bowl which then becomes a toucher.

The position of the jack or a toucher bowl in the ditch area must be marked as soon as it comes to rest. This is best done by first of all ensuring that the fender is in its correct position, then marking the carpet with three small chalk

*It's usual to place marks on the toucher bowl, just off the running surface on opposite sides, either with chalk or a chalk puffer. Marking both sides enables it to be verified without having to move the bowl should it be knocked over and a mark obscured.*

marks equidistant around the periphery of the bowl and/or jack, as close as possible without moving them. It makes replacing them into their original positions much easier if, for example, they have been moved by a non-toucher bowl. In a close game the accuracy of such a restoration can be crucial in determining the winner.

A line decision, to verify whether the jack or a bowl is in or out of play, can be called for at any time during an end. Similarly, any non-toucher found in the ditch or touching the ditch line can be removed at any time.

> *Driving the jack off the carpet, usually for tactical reasons, is perfectly legitimate, but note that there are a limited number of times you can do this without penalty, usually only once or twice in a match per team.*

## Foot-faulting

A foot-fault occurs if the trailing foot is not above or within the confines of the delivery mat, at the time that the bowl is released. It's also a foot-fault if the front foot is not inside the inner edges of the side lines (the delivery area) when the bowl is released.

No part of the body shall be in contact with the ditch area, fender, or any part of the carpet outside the legitimate delivery area. Except the bowling arm and bowl which may extend beyond the side lines during the delivery action.

When 'foot-fault' is called in singles, the marker must stop the bowl and remove it. In pairs, triples and fours games only the players involved at the delivery end, or the umpire, may call foot-faults; the opposing player at the other end who is in charge of the head shall stop the offending bowl and remove it.

In the circumstances where, following a foot-fault, or the bowl touching the centre block, a bowl impacts into the head and moves any of the other bowls, the opposing person in charge of the head should replace them where he/she thinks they were before they were moved; their decision is not open for discussion and must be considered final. In view of this, it must be emphasized that the players at the head should be ready to react quickly to try to stop any such displacements.

## 4. Measures and other equipment

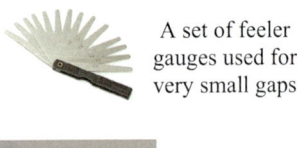 A set of feeler gauges used for very small gaps

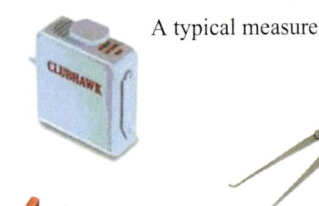 A typical measure

A set of wedges, used to stabilize a tilting bowl prior to measuring for shot bowl.

 A pair of calipers used to measure small gaps

A Rooney folding square

Distances between bowls and the jack that are in contention for shot bowl are usually determined by eye or, if there's any doubt, with a measure. If the differences are too close for a measure, calipers are used, or if very close, feeler gauges. Any dispute concerning a bowl that has infringed a defining line is resolved using a Rooney folding square.

*A measure consists of a spring loaded, 3m to 5m long tape or string coiled inside a small box with a simple locking mechanism. It is used for relative measurements between the bowl and the jack. The pointed projection on the case is positioned to just touch the centre of the jack and the tape is extended until it just touches the widest part of the bowl.*

*A Rooney folding square is a hinged device which is laid flat along the defining edge of the tape line adjacent to the bowl in question. The central hinged section is then raised and becomes an exact right angle. If this intersects in any way with the nearest side of the bowl, it is deemed to have crossed the line.*

The object of the game is to complete an end having one or more of your team's bowls nearer to the jack than any of your opponents' bowls. Every one of a team's bowls that are nearer than any of the other team's bowls, counts as a 'shot'.

# 5. Determining the winner

The total number of shots accumulated at the conclusion of the game determines the winner.

Many inter-club competitions require four teams to take part, two from each club but this can vary between different counties. Typically, clubs A and B have two teams of four players each. One team from each club plays the other, the winner of the game being awarded 2 points. The other two teams then play each other and the winner also gets 2 points. If a draw in either game, the points for that game are divided equally. Depending on the availability of carpets at a venue the games are usually played simultaneously.

The overall score is a maximum of 8 points: 2 for each game plus 4 for the team with the highest overall shot score. In the event of a draw in the final scores the 4 points are divided equally.

It does mean that although your club may have won one game, if the other club collectively scores more shots overall, they will win the match.

From this you'll see that although you may be losing your game, keeping the shot difference to a minimum may still save the day.

*During competitions, an umpire is appointed to ensure that the game is played to the rules and to resolve differences of opinion. In the absence of an umpire, a marker can be appointed to carry out any measuring requirements and to make line decisions. However, he or she isn't allowed to make any decisions concerning the rules, for example foot-fault or other default.*

*For singles matches, a marker is always required, mainly to position the jack at the request of the player concerned, to remove bowls outside the playing area and to answer legitimate questions. Usually the players measure for themselves and only if they can't agree is a third party called in to adjudicate. Quite often the marker will do it, providing both players agree.*

The score card shows the shot score and running total for each team after each end - in this case the game resulting in a draw, 11 shots all and 1 point each of the 2 points for the match. There are two cards like this for a match and the totals are added together to arrive at the total match score.

## 6. A typical score card

| ABC Short Mat Bowls Club | | | | |
|---|---|---|---|---|
| Versus **X Y Z** | | | | Bowls Club |
| Competition:  Local league | | | | Date  today |
| **HOME** | | **V** | **AWAY** | |
| J.  Bloggs | | **1** | A. Jones | |
| R. White | | **2** | C. Jones | |
| P.  Jenkins | | **3** | B. Brown | |
| E.  Bloggs | | **S** | C. Brown | |
| **Shots** | **Total** | **END** | **Shots** | **Total** |
| *1* | *1* | **1** | *0* | *0* |
| *1* | *2* | **2** | *0* | *0* |
| *3* | *5* | **3** | *0* | *0* |
| *0* | *5* | **4** | *2* | *2* |
| *0* | *5* | **5** | *4* | *6* |
| *1* | *6* | **6** | *0* | *6* |
| *2* | *8* | **7** | *0* | *6* |
| *0* | *8* | **8** | *1* | *7* |
| *0* | *8* | **9** | *2* | *9* |
| *0* | *8* | **10** | *2* | *11* |
| *1* | *9* | **11** | *0* | *11* |
| *2* | *11* | **12** | *0* | *11* |
| | *11* | **Score** | | *11* |
| | *1* | **Points** | *1* | |

Usually, at the conclusion of an end in a Fours game, the three who thinks he has the shot bowl/s will say "I am asking for 1 or 2 or 3 shots etc." depending on the number he thinks qualify. It is then up to the opposing three to either agree or to measure the relative distances between the jack and the bowls to clarify the situation.

## 7. Choice of Bowls

Bowls made of rubber or composition have a maximum diameter of 131mm and a minimum diameter of 116mm and the weight must not exceed 1.59kg. (3.5lbs.)

Bowls made of wood (lignum vitae) have a maximum diameter of 134mm and a minimum diameter of 116mm and the weight must not exceed 1.59kg.

An important choice is the bowl size. This in turn depends to a large extent on the size of the bowler's hands and their preference in the method of gripping the bowl. Handling comfort is usually the main consideration. Using the largest and heaviest bowl meeting that criteria, is the preferred option.

The metric/imperial size chart is basically self explanatory, although if you have an earlier set of bowls they may only have the inch dimensions shown rather than the bowl sizes - if they have anything at all. Some have grips and others are smooth. The latter should be avoided – grips give much better handling conditions.

| Dia. mm | Size | Dia. in |
|---------|------|---------|
| 116 | 00 | 4 9/16 |
| 117 | 0 | 4 5/8 |
| 121 | 1 | 4 3/4 |
| 122 | 2 | 4 13/16 |
| 124 | 3 | 4 7/8 |
| 125 | 4 | 4 15/16 |
| 127 | 5 | 5 |
| 129 | 6 | 5 1/16 |
| 131 | 7 | 5 1/8 |

Playing with unsuitable bowls will not help your game. If

you can't hold the bowl comfortably it's probably too big for your hand. Try a different set of bowls.

## 8. What does bias mean?

All bowls have an inbuilt bias which causes the bowl to follow a curved path. Whilst the bowl is traveling quickly the centrifugal force holds it upright and it will run in a straight line. As the speed drops the bias takes effect and it will start to turn. The amount of bias is determined by the contours of the running band (sole) of the bowl.

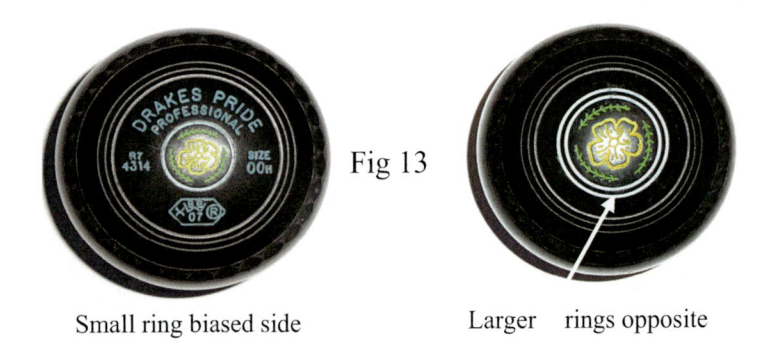

Fig 13

Small ring biased side        Larger    rings opposite

The biased side of the bowl is always defined by the smaller set of concentric rings on the side of the bowl.(Fig13) That is, the side of the bowl that turns inwards when the bowl starts to slow down.

The bowl is always held so that the biased side is towards the centre block when it is delivered – no matter whether you are left or right handed.

*It's not a good idea to rush into buying any bowls until you've tried out different sizes, weights, grips, etc. Most bowlers are very willing to let you borrow theirs for this purpose. Try as many as you can. Some bowls shops will let you try out two of a set of four of their bowls for a short period.*
*It's not uncommon for more experienced players to have more than one set of bowls so that they can select the type most suitable for the carpet concerned.*

**Choosing the size to suit you**.
As a general rule, if you can touch your two thumb tips together on one side of the running band and the middle fingers touch on the opposite side then it is probably ok. If your fingers overlap it is too small and if there is a gap between the finger tips it is too large. This is only a guide, the important point is that the bowl must be comfortable to hold without placing any undue strain on your wrist or hands.

Some short mat bowlers, having smaller hands, use a slightly larger and heavier bowl, by utilising the cradle grip.

There are a variety of biases. These give rise to different 'finishes' to the bowl's travel. i.e. some bowls take a path which curves less than others and/or the final amount of turn, or 'hook', is more pronounced. The choice of a narrow-line bowl versus a normal bias bowl is very much a personal one and should not be rushed.

It's worth noting that whilst narrow-line bowls may be better suited to a home carpet that has a very pronounced swing to it, they will not be so well suited to the majority of carpets that tend to run much straighter and could be a disadvantage when playing in away matches.

These features are well illustrated by the different Bowls manufacturers. It must be said that the similarities between different types of bowls are much greater than their differences.

*Although there's no requirement in short mat bowls for players to bowl with a matched set of bowls. In practice, most bowlers stick to one set of bowls at a time*

# 9. Forehand and backhand
If you're right-handed a forehand delivery will take your bowl to the right of the block. The forehand grip has the little finger placed nearest the side of the bowl with the smaller concentric ring - the biased side.

The backhand grip has the thumb positioned on the biased side and the bowl will roll past the left side of the block. Conversely, if you're left-handed a forehand delivery will pass to the left of the block, a back hand delivery will pass on the right side of the block.

This means that whichever side you're bowling on, the biased side is always on the inside of the drawing line for both left and right-handed bowlers. See also Section 13.

## 10. Gripping the bowl

There are two basic methods of gripping the bowl - the claw grip and the cradle grip.

### The claw grip

This grip (Figs 4 and 5) requires the thumb to be positioned either on the upper side or the top of the bowl. The fingers are placed underneath on the running surface of the bowl, neither the little finger nor the forefinger extending beyond the grip indentations. This grip is essentially with the finger and thumb tips which are the only parts of the hand in contact with the bowl. It should be possible to hold the bowl with the hand upside down without dropping it (Fig 5)

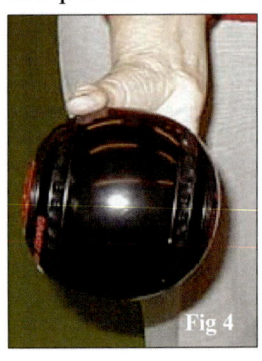
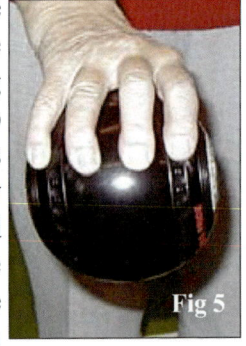

Fig 4

Fig 5

A damp chamois leather is a great help in keeping the hands slightly moist to assist the grip without having to hold the bowl too tightly which can cause tension to build up in the hand.

### The cradle grip

The cradle grip (Figs 6 and 7) enables those with smaller hands to hold bowls that might otherwise prove difficult with the claw grip. The bowl is placed in the palm of the hand with the thumb and fingers spread to each side. Its main disadvantage is that with heavier shots needing a longer

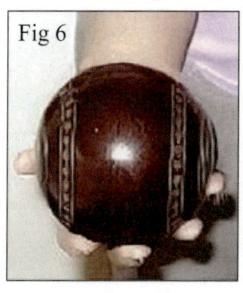

backswing, it may sometimes be necessary to articulate the wrist to prevent the bowl falling from the hand. If you can't hold the bowl

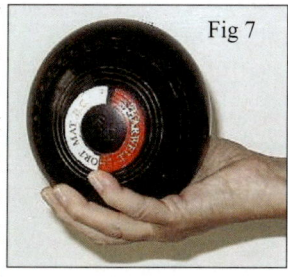

comfortably it's probably too big for your hand.

To assist your grip you could try 'Grippo' or 'Wilgrip' or some other type of non-slip wax polish. A little on the finger tips normally suffices. Another alternative is a mixture of glycerin and rose-water rubbed into the hands.

Whichever grip you use, always make sure that you hold the bowl the same way and you will go a long way towards a cure for any tendency to wobble or skew the bowl.

*For the **Claw grip** - You can use the grips to establish three firm, positive and repeatable registration points. The thumb on the top side grip, the forefinger underneath on the same side and the little finger underneath on the opposite side. Each secure in an indentation.*

*For the **Cradle grip** - It is still possible to ensure a repeatable method of holding the bowl by using the first and third fingers to register in the grips.*

Add to this a positive guidance from having your longest finger in the centre of the bowl and your accuracy will improve significantly. It should be the last point of contact when the bowl leaves your hand. If your follow-through is correct the chances are that your bowling line will also be correct. The main consideration is to be comfortable and not place any undue strain on the hands. White knuckles are a sure sign of tension often caused by gripping the bowl too tightly.

# 11. Stance on the delivery mat

## Semi-crouch stance

Start with your leading foot placed in front of and to the side of the delivery mat, within the limits of the white side delivery lines, and with the back foot placed completely within the confines of the mat (Fig 8). This is the position many short mat bowlers adopt. It tends to minimize the number of variables by providing a basically stable 'platform' from which to bowl. If you have difficulty holding this position then the upright stance may be more suitable.

Fig 8

## Upright stance

Start with both feet together on the delivery mat with relaxed knees and shoulders (Fig 9). Then take a short step forward with the left foot (or right foot, if left -handed) and bowl in a simultaneous and fluid movement. Starting from this position, the sequence is essentially the same as that shown in figs.10-13. as one continuous movement but from the initial short step

Take care to use only one hand to hold the bowl at the start of your delivery stance. The use of both hands tends to create a hooked delivery.

Fig 9

A smooth extended delivery will help you to achieve a follow-through which ensures that your arm and bowl travel through your aiming point. (See Section 13) this will also help to avoid twisting your hand, and subsequently the bowl.

There will be occasions when you'll have to modify this 'normal' delivery, for example when playing a backhand shot on a wide swinging carpet, (See Section 19)

## Long Step Stance

The importance of the delivery technique cannot be over emphasized. Many players take a 'long step' stance with their leading foot which enables a better balance to be obtained and also facilitates the long delivery action. The hand holding your bowl when in the initial sighting position should be approximately level with your right hip or a little higher (Fig 10). Then slowly swing your arm back to a point

Fig 10

Fig 11

level, or just behind, your right knee as you step forward. (See Fig 11) follow this with a controlled forward swing past the right hip with the release occurring around the side-front of your left foot - the objective being to set up the direction and pace of the delivery. (Fig 12) As you progress you'll find that your arm's delivery arc will increase and become a slow controlled movement from the shoulder. The pace of this delivery swing will assist you to get the length right. It helps if you maintain the same arm speed during the backswing and the forward delivery swing, culminating in a

Fig 12      Fig 13

positive follow-through action. (Fig 13) A slow backswing followed by a more rapid delivery swing can create instability and loss of control.

## 12. Delivery and follow-through

The previous section illustrates the three basic delivery methods. Whichever stance you adopt, the importance of the follow-through cannot be over emphasized. It determines the direction of the delivery. If the arm is held at the end of the delivery until the bowl is well on its way (as in Fig13) it's proper execution enables you to see the aiming point, the line taken and the result all in one go. This can be a great help for correcting future deliveries – or consolidating them. It's important that the angles of the elbow, wrist and fingers are aligned and maintained in a constant manner throughout the delivery action.

> *If your hand is palm up at the end of your follow-through you will not be able to hook your delivery.*

# 13. The aiming point

 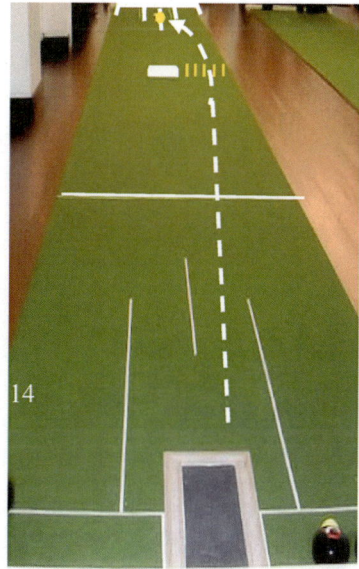

Fig 14

There are various methods of deciding the line you want your bowl to take. The one I prefer, is to imagine that there's a ruler between the end of the block and the edge of the carpet (See Fig 14).

Picture the curved line your bowl will take to get to the jack (or the position requested by your skip) The intersection of this line with a point along the imaginary 'ruler' becomes your aiming point. If your bowl goes too wide, visualize the intersecting point a little closer to the block and conversely, if it goes too narrow, move the intersection point out a little.

You've now established the aiming point although it will

*Try to avoid using a very wide drawing line where your bowl runs along the edge of the carpet as it's the most common cause of losing your bowl off the side. Generally it's best to try to bowl over the mid-point between the block and carpet edge, using appropriate feet positions on the delivery mat to compensate (Section 19).*

change with each carpet you play on, and sometimes from the other end as well.

Usually it's best to start with an aiming point in the centre of your 'ruler', noting the results carefully and adjusting accordingly at the next opportunity. Your objective is to ensure that your bowl travels precisely over your aiming point. You will not be looking anywhere else; concentrate on that specific spot right up to when you complete your follow-through.

Take care to keep your head still; lifting it before you have released the bowl can cause you to bowl too heavily or miss your aiming point. Dropping your head down just before your delivery makes you lose sight of your aiming point and lose your concentration. It's also a common cause of bowling short.

Having an aiming point well beyond the block can cause neck pains, especially if you adopt a crouching stance.

Whichever way you choose to stand on the delivery mat, concentration, imagination and consistency are the criteria to employ.

The distance you have to bowl is 'in the mind'. You'll find that by concentrating on the aiming point you'll also establish not only the line, but also the length, thereby achieving a perfect draw shot. You'll have noted the jack's position during the process of imagining the line your bowl will take to get to the jack (or the position requested by your skip) so there is no need to look at it again.

*One of the most powerful factors in your possession is your imagination. When you're really concentrating you'll see the line you want to take 'standing out' as if it's etched into the carpet. You know your bowl is going exactly where you want it to and you can see that small gap alongside the jack and envisage your bowl gently nudging up against it.*

Visualizing the likely path of a bowl to determine the delivery line and speed is important. Imagine the path your bowl will take, and in your mind's eye see it reaching the point you want it to get to. Feel your middle finger contact with the bowl as you release it. You'll find that as you progress, many of these aiming criteria will become automatic. An alternative is to mentally track the line back from the jack to the mat, see the 'shoulder of the draw line and aim for the intersection on the 'ruler'

Some players prefer to align their aiming point with one of the white lines on the carpet at the far end, and bowl directly to it, or to one side or the other according to how the carpet is playing.

Others prefer to use the angle of their front foot, first set to point along an imaginary line they feel is the correct one to determine the way the bowl should run, then to bowl along the side of that foot as a guide.

All have one thing in common, the need to concentrate and the time to establish this, if possible, is at the trial ends.

## 14. Trial ends

Trial ends, played before competitive games begin, usually involve each player playing two bowls from each end. The main purpose is to give visiting teams a chance to acquaint themselves with the pace of the carpet and the amount of 'turn' their bowls take. If you're playing in an away match it's a good time to observe carefully what your opponents do, ignoring those who have a poor or inconsistent technique.

*Occasions often arise where there are no trial ends. Then it's even more important to watch what all the other players do. On a strange carpet it's vitally important to find out the line and length characteristics as soon as possible, otherwise you can be six or more shots down in no time at all. Watch all the bowls as they're delivered and observe the lines taken..*

If they are competent bowlers they'll have determined the variables of their own carpet and established methods to circumvent them. Watch the line they take and if they avoid the backhand or forehand; look also at how they hold the bowl. For example if they hold the bowl so that the bias is delayed, or it's wobbling, it will affect the run of the bowl (see Section 20)

The selection of which bowls to use can be made up to and including, the last of the trial ends. After that, you must stay with your chosen bowls until the game is completed.

When coming to this decision bear in mind that you can always make a normal bias bowl run straighter, at least for a short distance (Section 20). You can't, however, make a narrow-line bowl turn as much as a normal bias bowl. Remember too that there's no requirement for you to play with a matched set of bowls.

## 15. Carpet speed and characteristics

The speed of the carpet and the degree of 'swing' that your bowl will follow for a normal draw shot will vary appreciably between different carpet manufacturers. You'll find that some carpets will allow your bowls to turn easily and others hardly at all. Quite often one side of the carpet can be seen to run much straighter than the other and some carpet/floor combinations tend to force a bowl to run against the bias, especially when a heavier shot is played.

Speed can be defined as the length of time it takes for the bowl to travel from the delivery mat to the centered jack with a drawing delivery. A fast carpet will have a bigger swing compared to a slow one and the time taken for a bowl to just reach the jack will be longer than a draw shot on a slow carpet where the bowl will take a straighter line and take less time to get there.

As this tends to be a little confusing it's probably best to think in terms of a heavy carpet being a slow one even if it does takes a narrower line.

Another significant factor is the floor beneath the carpet. Short mat bowling usually takes place at club level in village halls, town and school halls and the like, and consequently the floor levels can vary  significantly. All sorts of 'runs' and changes in the line the bowl takes can and do occur. Changes in room temperature and humidity also affect carpets.

Major competitions are often held at indoor  bowls rinks with the short mat carpets laid out on top of the existing surface. This can give ideal bowling conditions, rarely found elsewhere. However, placing carpets on top of  the existing bowls surface can result in them becoming somewhat slower because of the extra overall thickness. This doesn't always create the ideal conditions, but nevertheless it does provide consistency, resulting in very few runs or sudden quirks.

These are some of the circumstances you'll have to confront when visiting other clubs and learning to deal with them is part of the skills you'll acquire.

> *Short mat bowls is one of those rare sports where even in one's 70s it's still possible to play competitive games to a high standard. It's also a very social activity enjoyed by both sexes from the age of about 14 to 80 plus.*

# 16. Delivery errors

Problems with your delivery can be caused by a variety of factors at any stage of the delivery process - ranging from incorrect grip and stance to a flawed action and faulty release. Two of the more common problems  are described here.

## Wobbling bowls

A ball that wobbles during its delivery is usually a sign of misalignment of your grip on the bowl and/or incorrect alignment of your hand or arm. Even a correctly aligned bowl will wobble if wrist or finger movement occurs during delivery, or if you apply force other than through the centre of the bowl.

Wobble is an unstable condition that generally dampens out whilst a bowl is running. A driven bowl might wobble until it strikes its target or reaches the ditch. The slower the delivery the faster the wobble dissipates.

| tilted | centred | skewed |

Fig 15

While wobble persists, it effectively reduces the offset of the bowl's centre of gravity, consequently wobbling bowls turn less than normal. In either case the bowl is likely to begin it's course either off square (skewed) or tilted, See Fig.15. To prevent this, the hand and wrist must be in alignment with the forearm. It may feel strange at first but persevere, until it feels natural

The last joint of the longest (usually the middle) finger should be positioned on the centre of the running surface, or 'sole' of the bowl and the tip of that finger should be the last point of contact when its released. If not, the bowl can skew off its intended delivery line. Implementing these corrections will ensure that the force that's finally imparted will be transmitted through the centre of the bowl and will prevent skewing of the delivery.

It's worth mentioning here that some outdoor bowlers new to the short mat version may find their bowls going off the side of the carpet, and this is nearly always due to an incorrect grip or delivery action. What you can get away with outdoors because: you are using body weight and because the bowl has much further to travel, simply won't work in the shorter game.

## Late release

Releasing your bowl late will cause it to bounce (Fig 16) If you're standing correctly you'll release the bowl alongside your front foot so that it's just touching the carpet at the point of release.

Fig 16

If however, you extend your hand beyond your foot before you release it, the swing of your arm will begin to lift the bowl away from the carpet and you'll inevitably drop it when it's released.

This often results in lunging just as you release the bowl to try and stop it bouncing and it's likely to causes a loss of line and/or length control. If you find this difficult to overcome, try lengthening the initial step.

The only other cause for dropping the bowl is simply that you're not near enough to the floor, so bend your knees more!

You can't expect to have a short-arm drawing style even if it sometimes works on a familiar carpet and then deliver an extended forcing or even a firing shot in the same way. This is particularly the case if you're used to a fairly fast carpet and then go to a slower one where you need to 'push' the bowl that much more anyway.

Short arm movements, wrist or finger flicks are much harder to keep consistent. Without consistency it's very much more difficult to make measured adjustments to line and length.

> *A controlled and systematic delivery is the basis of all the shots that you'll need to build into your armoury.*

## 17. Advanced shots

Even if you're a relative newcomer to short mat bowls it won't take you long to realize that in many situations the draw shot is inadequate to achieve your objective. This section looks at a number of advanced shots that, with practice, will help you to cope with the majority of situations that will arise. Many of them depend upon an understanding of how bowls react when they collide. Those who play snooker or billiards will have a head start!

This Section has examples of shots that can be made from the normal stance, delivery and grip, while Sections19 and 20 require changes to feet positions on the delivery mat and/ or your bowls grip respectively.

### The trail shot

For this shot your bowl will need to take a slightly narrower line than the drawing shot. Generally speaking, the faster the bowl travels to a given spot, the narrower the line. Imagine that you are trying to get your bowl to a position beyond the jack and to take the jack with it. Fig17 shows your (blue) bowl just  before it hits the jack. With the right pace, both bowl and jack will move to a position close to your other bowl behind the jack, scoring two shots.

Fig 17

You must visualize the line you would take in order to draw to the position beyond and 'through' the jack. As it has further to go, you must use just a little more force and the line will therefore be marginally narrower. Quite often the extra force you use is quite small and is done by 'thinking it' rather than consciously employing it. Just 'see' the bowl going that little bit further.

*Bear in mind that 2½ turns of a size 5 bowl travels almost exactly one metre.*

## The forcing or firing shot

This is used when the object is to take out or promote a bowl. It's essentially similar to but more forceful than the trail shot and consequently requires a narrower line. This usually means only an inch or two less than the drawing line. You won't require massive changes, just subtle ones. It requires a good deal of skill and accuracy to deliver a successful firing shot. The penalty for missing is at best a lost bowl and worse, destroying your own shots in the head.

*When about to play a heavy or firing shot you are obliged to visually signal and to call out clearly "playing up" or "weight on mat X" where X denotes the carpet on which you're playing. Warn those at the head and on nearby carpets as the shot must not be played until this has been done. Those at the head must take up defensive positions to prevent bowls leaving the carpet area altogether. They should also ensure that neighbouring players are aware.*

# 18. What happens when bowls collide

On contact, the energy in a moving bowl is transmitted into the stationary bowl and it's important to know how this happens and the effect it causes. Assume the object bowl is touching another bowl, when the moving bowl hits the object one, the energy is transmitted straight through the object bowl into the second one. If they're in line, the object bowl will remain virtually where it is and the second one will move away in a line opposite the impact point. see Fig 18 below

The parameters are basic - hit the bowl dead on and it will go in a straight line opposite the point of impact. Your bowl will largely remain where it was when it struck the object bowl because virtually all the energy in it has been transmitted into the other bowl. (sometimes called a chop and lie shot)

Hit the object bowl at an angle and it will travel in a line opposite to the point of impact but your bowl will deflect sideways. If you hit the side of the object bowl it will move sideways something less than 90 degrees. The nearer to 90 degrees of angle, the more force required to move the object bowl any distance. If you want several bowls to move you will need even more force.

> *Even a small bowl weighs in excess of 2½ pounds (1.13 kg) so the inertia of several bowls virtually touching is considerable.*

## The plant shot

The plant shot is an option where two bowls are touching or almost touching and in line with the jack. Striking the nearer (opponent's) bowl (Fig 18) will send your bowl straight to a position nearer to the jack. An important factor here is that it doesn't much matter where you strike the first bowl, because if they are touching, the energy will transmit through the point of contact into the

Opponents bowl

Fig 18

adjacent bowl. However, the greater the angle, the less the transmitted force to the object bowl.

Once you have grasped this basic principle it's not difficult to imagine what will happen, even to a second or third bowl beyond the object bowl. The main thing to remember is that the energy will always be transmitted through the target bowl to a point opposite the impact point of each successive bowl.

## The jack-plant

The jack can also be used to impart energy into a touching bowl (Fig 19) but because of its lower mass, less energy will be transmitted if it's not actually touching. It can be considered in the same way as a plant shot. Your bowl, on striking your other bowl (just short of the jack) will transmit its energy through the jack and cause the opponent's bowl to spring away. The jack will move forward a

Jack moves to about

Your bowl

Fig 19

little, as will your bowl and if the weight of your shot is not too heavy, will result in you getting shot bowl.

## The split

A classic example of bowls colliding to your advantage is the split (Fig 20) where two bowls are either side of but in front of the jack and close enough together so that another bowl cannot pass through the gap. A running bowl delivered precisely into the split between them will cause both the bowls to move away an equal amount and in so doing will absorb most

Fig 20

of the kinetic energy within the delivered bowl, bringing it to a stop on or near the jack. Even if the split is not exact you will still gain an advantage and be unlucky not to end up closer to the jack.

## The 'wick' or deflected bowl

Hitting another bowl at an angle (Fig 21) will not only cause it to move away, but will deflect your bowl as well. Here the angles are a little more difficult to foresee. Basically, the angle of deflection is equal to the angle of impact. That is to say if you hit the object bowl at say 7 o'clock your bowl will deflect at an angle at or about 10 o'clock. Providing

Fig 21

you get the weight of the shot right, you'll achieve the desired result. Much can be written about the effect of striking other bowls and it's a good idea to practice these shots.

Some carpets, tend to run straighter than others and your only real option is to use the bowls that are already there by deflecting off them, to gain the positions you want. Always consider the percentage advantages, or disadvantages, when deciding what to do and take into consideration the characteristics of the carpet you are playing on. As a last resort, if you can't see a direct connection or relationship between adjacent bowls and an obscured jack, try a firing 'hit and hope' shot. Better still, for the three (or the two in triples) to do it, the object being to get the jack out where the skip can see it and possibly 'save the end'.

## 19. Using the delivery mat

The new bowler should concentrate on achieving the desired line and length from the normal mat delivery position which is in its centre, (Fig 22) taking care to maintain the central aiming point by the block as far as possible.

Once these objectives have been attained with a reasonable level of consistency, you can try different feet positions on the delivery mat and attempt more difficult shots.

Fig 22

## Modifying your delivery

A number of situations can arise where your delivery needs to be modified to compensate for an obstructing bowl, or the jack has been displaced to the side of the carpet, or a floor/carpet combination that produces unusual bowling lines. Because of this it's important that the position of your feet on the delivery mat be considered as well. A carpet with an excessive swing can rarely be compensated for by the width of your aiming point from the centre block alone. To adjust for these conditions try the following options.

## The swinging backhand

Stand with your right foot in the centre or on the right side of the delivery mat and your left foot towards the right of the delivery area. (Fig 23) Then, by delivering the bowl from the inside of the front foot, you'll tend to 'use up' some of the swing before your bowl gets to the block - see the red dotted line in Fig 24.

In some more extreme cases, you can deliver the bowl from well

Fig 23

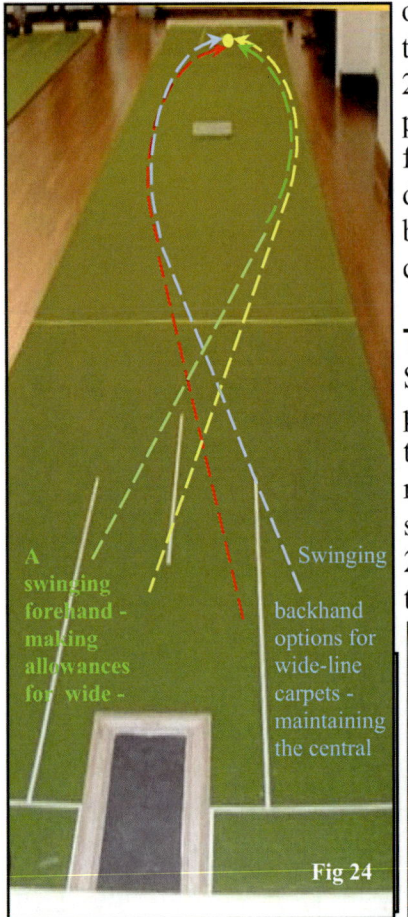

A swinging forehand - making allowances for wide -

Swinging backhand options for wide-line carpets - maintaining the central

**Fig 24**

outside the delivery line, eg. the dotted blue line in Fig 24. Make sure to be particularly careful that your front foot is between the delivery lines and at least, to begin with, maintain the central aiming point.

## The swinging forehand

Stand with your left foot positioned at the left side of the delivery area and your right foot in the centre or left side of the delivery mat (Fig 25). This stance will ensure that you deliver the bowl

Fig 25

starting from the inside of your front foot, and you will again 'use up' some of the swing before the block is reached. Imagine the path your bowl will take and in your mind's eye see it reaching its destination and feel your middle finger contact on the bowl as you release it.

The path of the bowl is shown as the dotted yellow line in Fig 24.

## The narrow backhand

It's sometimes necessary to deliver a running bowl close to the block on the backhand and it can be a very effective shot, for example to remove a shot bowl from alongside the jack

For this shot you should stand with your front foot as close to the side line as you can and your trailing foot close to the edge of the delivery mat on the same side (Fig 26) You then deliver the bowl from in front of your front foot, essentially bowling down the white line and close to the block. Make sure that you keep your head still and concentrate on your

Fig 26

aiming point - usually, just missing the block. If you remember that most of your weight will be on the front foot, it's not too difficult to maintain your balance.

## The reverse bias shot

A somewhat more specialist shot employed either on the forehand or the backhand, usually by Skips when faced with difficult situations. It means you are bowling with effectively less than half the width of the carpet. The objective being to deliver the bowl from a position as far out to the side as you can comfortably stand, making sure that one foot is on the mat and the other within the delivery

Fig 27

lines. Then bowl to just miss the block, using the opposite bias to that normally used. i.e. with the small rings on the outside of the bowl.

The bowl will travel towards the centre of the mat then back out to the same side again. It is a difficult shot and requires lots of practice. In the illustration shown (Fig 28) the jack cannot be reached with a normal backhand or forehand delivery, or even a firing shot because of the opposing bowls.

The Reverse-bias delivery can then be used when you want to either reach the jack, or strike the opponent's bowl in such a way as to deflect it to a safe position away from the jack. It's a shot which tends to be delivered with a little extra weight.

One of the more difficult aspects is to keep the weight down to that sufficient to hold the line without driving the jack off the carpet. Unless of course you want to!. Perhaps to destroy the head for tactical reasons.

Alternatively it can be used very effectively as a firing shot,

*The normal practice of leading with your left leg (for right-handed bowlers) can be reversed, that is leading with the right leg if it helps to free up a delivery, perhaps for a weighted shot needing a longer back swing or, for example, a reverse bias shot, to improve your balance. Another way to overcome what would otherwise be an awkward delivery is to bowl with your 'wrong' hand, that is with your left hand if you are right-handed and vice versa. Unless you're ambidextrous it's a difficult shot requiring much practice.*

to minimise the risk of driving into the head when it is intended to take out a bowl at the side of the head.

## 20. Using the bias for a purpose

You can of course, grip the bowl to use the bias to your advantage. Some bowlers grip the bowl in a skewed position

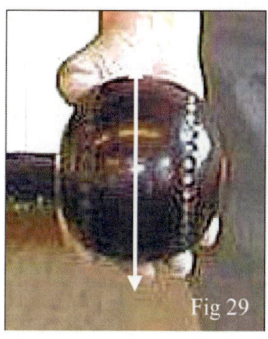

for delivering a drive thereby forcing it to wobble which makes their bowl follow a straighter line.

The bias built into the running

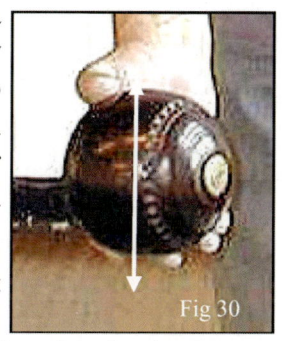

surface of a bowl only takes effect when it's beginning to slow down. If it's wobbling about its centre line axis this action is delayed until the wobbling diminishes to the extent that the bias can take effect. To do this you'll need to grip the bowl in its normal position in your hand with the bowl upright i.e. the running surface on top and level. (Fig 29) Then turn the bowl in your hand so that the running surface is skewed at an angle to the delivery line (Fig 30) Now bowl it as though you're holding it in its normal position bearing in mind that your aiming point may have to be slightly modified to assist the adjustment

This technique can also be used to overcome problems with uneven floors creating a situation whereby the carpet appears to have a bias of its own.

### Avoiding a short bowl

There can be occasions when it's not possible to draw past a short bowl using a normal delivery, even from an exaggerated starting point. This problem can be got round sometimes by delaying the point at which the bias on your bowl starts to take effect. It's achieved by again holding your bowl in its normal position in your hand, then tilting the

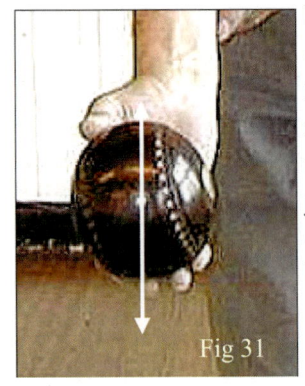

Fig 31

bowl sideways a little so that it runs diagonally across the edges of the running surface instead of along its middle track (Fig 31) This will cause the bowl to run in a straight line for just a little longer than would be the case with a normal centered grip, before the bias takes over, hopefully long enough for you

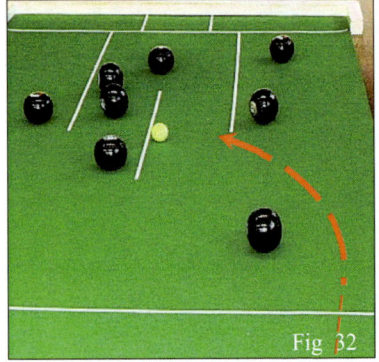

Fig 32

to pass the obstructing bowl before it turns into the head (Fig 32). The angle you turn the bowl is such that its top will always be inclined towards the outer edge of the carpet, whether you are using backhand or forehand.

## 21. Some what ifs
### You keep hitting the block!

If you keep hitting the block it's because you have either not concentrated on rolling your bowl over your aiming point or that aiming point is too near to the block.

Make sure that you deliver the bowl so that it rolls over the middle of the gap between the block and the edge of the carpet.

Change your starting point to compensate for a swinging bowling line.

Alternatively, you're not delivering the bowl correctly, check your hand/wrist/arm alignment and make sure you're delivering your bowl smoothly from the shoulder.

## Your bowl goes off the side of the carpet.

This is usually because you're not gripping the bowl properly or not delivering the bowl over the correct aiming point. Make sure your middle finger is directing the bowl.

Another possibility is that your bowl is very close to the edge of the carpet and wobbling, which can also take it off the carpet. Re-adjust your position on the delivery mat and/or your aiming point.

## You keep ending up in the ditch

Your delivery is too heavy. You must slow your delivery arm down and make your follow-through more deliberate. Try aiming short of the jack and combine this with a slower, more controlled delivery.

## You can't reach the far dead line

You're simply not bowling your bowl so try increasing your follow-through to make your shot more positive.

Stand at the front of the delivery mat, rather than the back of it and imagine your bowl traveling to the target.

> *Quite often the extra force you use is quite small and is done by 'thinking it' rather than consciously employing it. Just 'see' the bowl going that little bit further.*

## 22. Ups and downs
### When things aren't going well

Carry out the following mental check by asking yourself these questions:

- Are you relaxed?
- Are you holding your bowl correctly?
- Are your hand and fingers in line with your forearm?
- Is your delivery and follow-through taking your hand though your aiming point?
- Are you standing on the correct part of the delivery mat for the shot you're trying to make?
- Is your hand or arm twisted as you release your bowl?

## Things to make you better

Be constantly aware of
- Your grip - keep it constant
- Are you gripping the bowl too tightly?
- Target point - keep it central between the block and the edge of the carpet
- Starting point - move it to maintain your target point
- Follow-through - ensure you do it and end with your palm facing upwards
- Concentration - essential you maintain it
- Option to try skewed or tilted shots as a last resort

# 23. How to improve

## Practice

Regular, purposeful practice is the best way to attain proficiency and the first and most important factor is to achieve consistency in the draw shot. Practise it with an exaggerated follow-through to start with. Don't be concerned if your shots seem to be too long at first as you'll soon adjust the speed of your delivery arm to compensate.

If you find that you're bowling a little too long, try lowering your hand from the initial sighting position an inch or two. This automatically reduces the back swing without you being consciously aware of it.

As far as possible, make sure that you're bowling through your central aiming point, adjusting the position of your feet if necessary to accomplish this.

You'll develop a smooth, fluid style quite quickly. The forcing shots will then become an extension of that delivery style and require very little extra effort.

*The English Short Mat Bowling Association has a very good set of 16 basic skills exercises on its website at http://esmba.co.uk/*

## Handling pressure

You can't practise handling pressure - experience it and gain confidence. This means entering competitions and/or playing in league matches. If you play for your County it gets worse - and better! Develop a positive state of mind, self-belief and a will to win. Some people actually thrive under pressure. Be prepared to eat, drink and rest when you can.

Take a bottle of water with you to prevent dehydration. Some fruit pastilles or other sugar boost can be helpful too. Put pressure on the opposition by making them play the difficult shots and remain relaxed yourself.

# 24. Positional play

This section discusses the playing role of the members in a team, each one having a significant contribution to make towards the overall team effort. Some of their other duties, such as scoring, are outlined in Sect. 26

## The lead

Before the first bowl is delivered leads should ensure that the fender has its shorter ends in line with the determining edge of the ditch line and that the mat is correctly placed between the delivery mat lines with the short end in contact with the fender.

It's usual for leads to choose the hand on which they prefer to deliver the bowl, but they should be prepared for skips to direct otherwise.

Strategically, it's important for leads to get those first bowls close to the jack, ideally just behind or immediately in front of it. It provides a psychological boost for the whole team.

Bowls that are at the side of the jack form a bigger target and present a 'shoulder' that can be used by the opposition. If you do get your first one alongside the jack, make use of it yourself to get the next one on target.

If the draw to the jack is easier on one side, as far as possible make sure that you get there first and force your opponents onto the other hand.

Don't worry about bowls that run through a 30cm (1 foot) or so behind the jack as they can often be useful as the game progresses. Short obstructing bowls however, are the bane of every skip's life.

## The two
The two's job is to help build the head, so the ability to place the bowl where it's wanted is a vital part of their game. They are also responsible for keeping the score - See Scoring on page 46.

Skips will indicate where they would like the bowls to finish. If the lead hasn't succeeded in getting close to the jack, the two must try to get the shot bowl. Always remember that the skip is developing a strategy concerning the build-up of the head and may ask for a bowl to be positioned away from the immediate head.

## The three (or two in triples)
Threes have a key role within the team with the primary task of consolidating the head. Accordingly, they should be capable of playing all the shots, from precise positional play to removing an opponent's bowl when asked.

Threes should assess the head continuously and if it's changed significantly should advise the skip who may then ask for their opinion as to which shot to play. The three must therefore be able to 'read the head' (Section 25) to understand that the obvious draw shot may not be the best approach. He should try and anticipate what the opposing skip may do. For example, a better outcome may require that an opponent's bowl be moved, thus bringing one or more of their own team's bowls into the count.

Quite often there are other alternatives and the three must

recognize them and be prepared to advise the skip accordingly. Answers to the skip's questions should be short, concise and positive so a cool head and sound judgment are essential prerequisites.

Subject to local rules, the laws of short mat bowls allow team members to change positions during a game so, if asked, threes should be capable of taking over from their skip or any other position. Finally, as a three it's crucial to remain positive and supportive of your skip and to remember that the skip asks and the three tells.

*The three (or two in triples) should have immediate access to wedges, also known as chocks (for supporting any leaning bowls), a measure and/or calipers, and feeler gauges for comparing the distance between adjacent bowls and the jack.*

## The skip

The skip's job is to lead their team - to encourage, cajole, entreat or persuade, but never to censure or reprimand. Telling a team member they are useless is not going to make them try any harder. Avoid all negative remarks like "Don't be short" or "Don't do that", choose positive comments instead.

At the start of each end the skip places the jack somewhere along the length of the central jack line. Where they put it is a matter of tactics and is their decision alone, but there's no point in always putting it in the centre if the opposition's lead finds it easy to bowl to and your own lead has difficulties.

During the course of a match is not the time for teaching or instruction. The skip can perhaps suggest a different starting position on the delivery mat, or if a player is consistently bowling too long, advise that they slow their follow-through a little or bowl to a shorter target. This can best be done with a quiet word or two when changing over during an end.

When directing the team, skips should be positive, brief and avoid alternatives as they usually confuse! Ending up in two minds usually means that neither option is achieved. Finally, remember that the skip is in sole charge of the team. With their opposing skip they will decide all disputed points or shots. When both agree, their decision is final, if they cannot agree one or the other may call the umpire

## The team

It's very important that every member of the team should be fully supportive of each other at all times. Those at the head mustn't move when a player is about to deliver their bowl and once it has come to rest, remember that possession of the delivery mat passes to the other team.

It's bad sportsmanship to talk intrusively whilst your opponent is delivering their bowl. However, it's perfectly permissible to congratulate a team member after they've played a good shot as it encourages a good team spirit.

If you're the lead or the two and your skip asks a question concerning the head, don't butt in, the three will answer.

If you're the skip, don't interfere with the threes when they're determining the shot-bowl. It's their job and only when they can't agree do the two skips intervene.

When skips leave the head to deliver their own bowls they will have a clear idea of what they want to achieve and which shot they want to play. Placing a critical bowl requires complete concentration and anything which destroys that concentration, such as sudden movements or offering last minute advice just before the skip bowls, is usually disastrous. Expecting skips to save the end in such circumstances is unrealistic.

Gratuitous advice by anyone should be avoided since no one wants to deliver a bad bowl and if it does happen, and it will, remember, you may be the next one to do so.

If it's your opponent's mat, only their player is allowed on it. All the remaining players should stand behind the fender. After the end is finished and when counting the shots, only the two threes are allowed on the carpet (or the twos in triples)

It's courteous to commend a good bowl from your opponent, without going overboard about it. Concede a fluke in good spirit and don't blame the carpet, the floor or other conditions if you lose; the victor had exactly the same conditions to contend with.

Allow your opponents time to congratulate you if you win, but never fail to thank them for the game.

## 25. Reading the head

Reading the head may be defined as 'examining the position of the jack and all the bowls around it (the head) and assessing all possible consequences of the next and if possible, subsequent deliveries'

The objective, of course, is to build up the head to maximize the chances of winning the end or, failing that, ensuring that an adverse position doesn't deteriorate.

Reading the head is a skill that comes with experience, so although much can be written about this subject it must be appreciated that this book is mainly designed for those starting out and developing their game. However, it's felt that one or two thoughts here won't come amiss in making newcomers aware of some of the issues involved.

As a skip you must not only be able to lead your team tactically through skilled head-building judgment, but you must also be able to anticipate what the opposing skip is trying to achieve.

For example, if two of your own bowls are situated either side of and in front of the jack (Fig 20) the opposing skip will want his bowl to split them and probably take shot bowl. Your defense is either to get one of your own team's bowls immediately behind that pair, or better still, just in front of the split position to block the split shot, thus minimizing the possible damage.

Again, if one of your teams bowls is short and directly in  the draw line of your opponent it's usually a good idea to leave it there. It will stop the opponent drawing directly to the jack and if they do try there's a good chance that they'll promote your bowl towards the jack.

If you're holding shot bowl and most of your opponent's bowls are behind the jack, make sure that you have a bowl or two amongst them, because if the opposing skip runs the jack back and you have nothing there, you'll be in trouble.

In triples the skip usually keeps the score card and  also agrees the shot or shots with the opposing skip, the lead and two having enough to do in moving the bowls back to the fender and setting up the delivery mat.

## 26. Scoring

### e.g. in a fours game

One of the key duties of the twos is to keep the score cards. They should  ensure that the players' names in both teams are entered on the score card.

After each end they record the score, and  also compare their card with the  opposing two. They should retain the score card at all times and hand it to their skip on completion of the game. The home two is also responsible for keeping the  rink score marker up to date.

The practice of having the score card maintained by a spectator isn't a satisfactory one as it doesn't allow the opposing two a chance to compare scores. Moreover, in the case of a dispute, a spectator's score card will be disallowed.

The three's role in scoring is to measure bowls in contention for shot, allowing the opposing three to do the same if they wish and to agree between themselves the number of shots.
They also ensure that their two has the score recorded. If they can't agree, the respective skips will be asked to arbitrate. In practice, where Umpires are available they are asked to intervene. They must also keep their skip informed.
Threes also mark all touchers, and if necessary, delete marks from non-touchers, They also remove any dead bowls from the carpet or ditch.

## A Triples game
The two proves the claim for shots by measuring, but won't move any bowl until the shot or shots are agreed, allowing the opposing two to also measure if required. If the twos can't agree, they call the skips to arbitrate.

The two chalks all touchers, deletes chalk marks left on any non-touchers and also removes any dead bowls from the carpet or ditch.

## 27. Bowls stamping
Unless your bowls are very old they will each carry a stamp that contains letters and numbers similar to the one illustrated here. Over the years the shape of the stamp has changed, but the one shown here introduced by World Bowls in 2002, is the most recent.

The meaning of the characters is as follows:
The 'A' is the code letter of the licensed manufacturer or licensed tester, each company having a different letter, for example:

A = Thomas Taylor;
N = Henselite;
V = Greenmaster;
X = Drakes Pride.

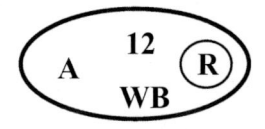

The letters WB stand for World Bowls - the recognized international federation for the sport of bowls. The R shows that the stamp is a registered trade mark. The 12 refers to the year that the stamp expires, in this case 2012. The stamp indicates that the bowl conforms to regulations laid down by bowls authorities of those codes recognized by the English Short Mat Bowling Association, essentially in respect of size, weight and bias.

## 28. In summary

Short mat bowls requires a minimum amount of equipment without any great financial outlay. Most clubs charge only a small amount to join and annual fees are usually low.

The minimum age for playing short mat bowls depends mostly on being big enough to grasp a suitable bowl and having the self-discipline to control bad behaviour. Generally, from about 14 onwards.

When you start playing short mat bowls your expectations will probably range from contentment at occasional social level to ambitions at club, county or even country level. Whatever your aspirations, improvement typically goes hand in hand with increasing enjoyment.

At the social level, your development will stem from playing more often, perhaps every week instead of fortnightly, and who knows - perhaps your progress will lead to entry into club competitions and beyond.

For those with higher aims, the cornerstones of advancement are based on a sound delivery technique coupled with adequate purposeful practice and increasing levels of competition.

A good basic draw shot will enable you to develop your repertoire of shots without having to unlearn bad habits, whilst purposeful practice will provide the yardstick for self-evaluation and competition will hone your tactical skills and psychological strengths.

# About the author

Roy Wiggins lives in Oxfordshire and has been married for over 54 years with three sons, 9 grandchildren and 6 great-grandchildren. He left school in 1944 to become an apprentice with 'The Gramophone Company' in Hayes, Middlesex.

In 1946 he joined the Royal Navy as a boy telegraphist and served in various ships and shore establishments around the world, including a 2½ year commission in the West Indies on the cruiser, HMS *Glasgow*.

He left the Navy in 1959 to join the aircraft industry for several years before switching initially to the machine tool industry and then as MD of his own company, retiring in 1994.

Taking up flat green bowling at Esso Bowling Club in 1990 he became captain in 1996, a position he held for the next three years. The club changed its name to Milton Hill Bowling Club in 1999 and was officially opened on a new site in 2003.

He set up the Milton Hill web site in 2002 which includes an online bowls book covering the fundamentals of the outdoor game. Later he created another web site for one of his other interests, freemasonry, and now maintains both sites.

Cutting back on the outdoor game because of knee problems in 1999, he started playing the less strenuous game of short mat bowls at the Harwell Short Mat Bowls Club. His experience outdoors stood him in good stead and he quickly adapted and became a regular skip.

After unsuccessfully searching the web and elsewhere to find any books on short mat bowls, an enforced lull following a knee replacement gave him time to set about writing his first book. Now, after a second knee replacement, he's able to continue with league games and has taken the opportunity to update and enhance his first book .

He's now been able to continue outdoor lawn bowling as well as the short mat game and finds no confliction - the two games actually enhance each other.

Because of the generally much tighter heads in the short mat game the expectations in the outdoor version are raised, and in particular the need to control the hand, grip and arm alignment in the short mat game helps to improve the outdoor game.

More recently he has qualified as an England Bowls Coach for lawn bowls and coaches regularly at both his own outdoor bowling club and the West Berks Indoor Bowling Club in Newbury.

Lightning Source UK Ltd.
Milton Keynes UK
UKRC022055291018
331425UK00001B/11